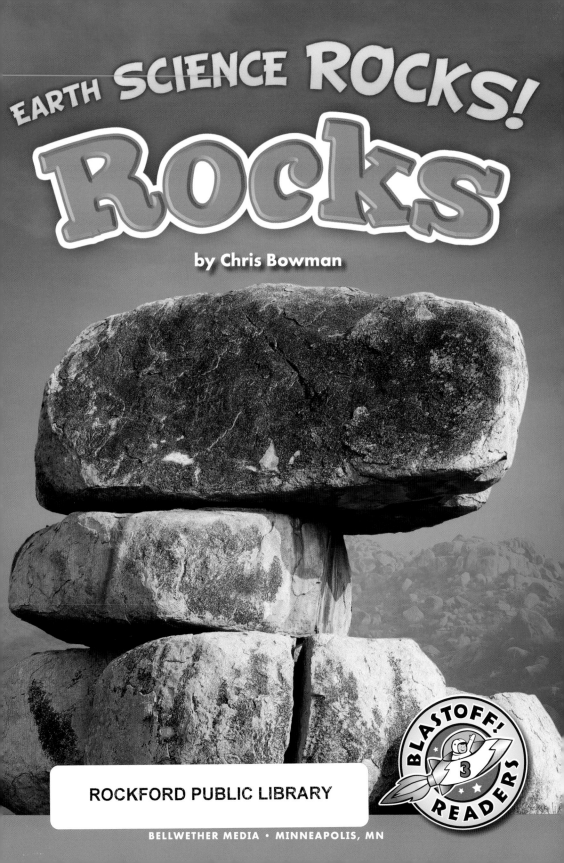

EARTH SCIENCE ROCKS!

Rocks

by Chris Bowman

BLASTOFF! READERS

3

BELLWETHER MEDIA • MINNEAPOLIS, MN

Note to Librarians, Teachers, and Parents:

Blastoff! Readers are carefully developed by literacy experts and combine standards-based content with developmentally appropriate text.

Level 1 provides the most support through repetition of high-frequency words, light text, predictable sentence patterns, and strong visual support.

Level 2 offers early readers a bit more challenge through varied simple sentences, increased text load, and less repetition of high-frequency words.

Level 3 advances early-fluent readers toward fluency through increased text and concept load, less reliance on visuals, longer sentences, and more literary language.

Level 4 builds reading stamina by providing more text per page, increased use of punctuation, greater variation in sentence patterns, and increasingly challenging vocabulary.

Level 5 encourages children to move from "learning to read" to "reading to learn" by providing even more text, varied writing styles, and less familiar topics.

Whichever book is right for your reader, Blastoff! Readers are the perfect books to build confidence and encourage a love of reading that will last a lifetime!

This edition first published in 2015 by Bellwether Media, Inc.

No part of this publication may be reproduced in whole or in part without written permission of the publisher. For information regarding permission, write to Bellwether Media, Inc., Attention: Permissions Department, 5357 Penn Avenue South, Minneapolis, MN 55419.

Library of Congress Cataloging-in-Publication Data

Bowman, Chris, 1990- author.
  Rocks / by Chris Bowman.
     pages cm. – (Blastoff! Readers. Earth Science Rocks!)
  Summary: "Developed by literacy experts for students in kindergarten through grade three, this book introduces rocks to young readers through leveled text and related photos"– Provided by publisher.
  Audience: Age 5-8.
  Audience: Grade K to grade 3.
  Includes bibliographical references and index.
  ISBN 978-1-60014-981-8 (hardcover : alk. paper)
  1. Rocks–Collection and preservation–Juvenile literature. I. Title.
  QE433.6.B69 2014
  552–dc23
                                    2014006615

Printed in the United States of America, North Mankato, MN.

Table of Contents

What Are Rocks?

Rocks are **solids** made up of **minerals**. They can be big like mountains or small like pebbles. Rocks make up much of Earth.

How Rocks Form

granite

marble

limestone

Granite, marble, and limestone are all rocks. However, each one is a different type. They are made by different natural processes.

Earth's Layers

Earth is made up of the inner core, outer core, mantle, and crust. Rocks are found in the mantle and crust.

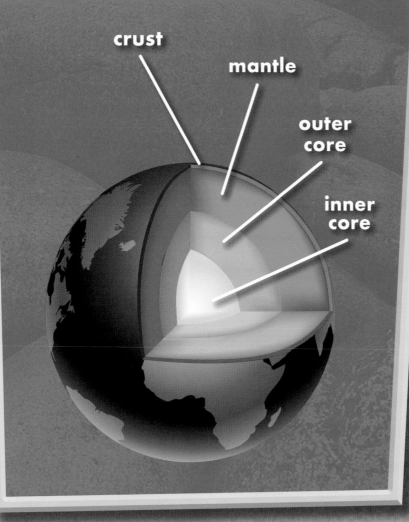

crust

mantle

outer core

inner core

Types of Rocks

Igneous rocks form when hot liquid from **volcanoes** cools. Some form underground from cooled **magma**. These are called **plutonic rocks**. Granite is an example.

granite

plutonic rocks

Rock Cycle

igneous rock

magma
crystallization

weathering /
erosion

magma

sediment

metamorphic
rock

sedimentary
rock

Other igneous rocks are made by **lava**. This **erupts** out of a volcano. Then it cools and hardens into **volcanic rocks**. This is how basalt forms.

basalt

Sedimentary rocks form when **sediments** collect in an area. This is often at the bottom of a body of water or in a desert. Pressure crushes the deepest bits to form rocks such as limestone.

limestone

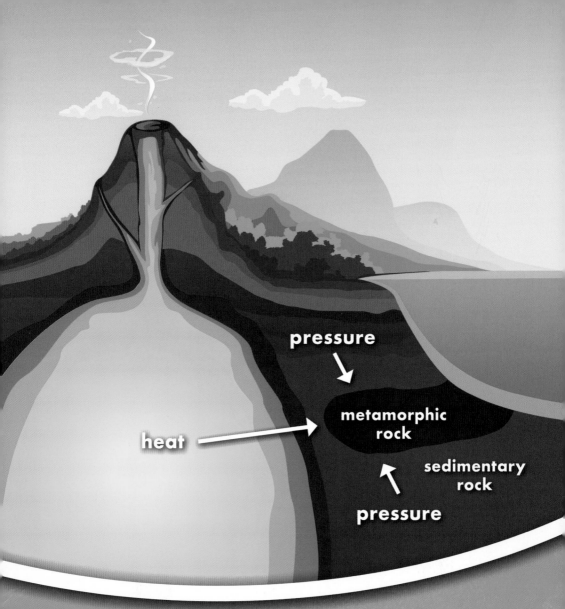

Heat and pressure turn igneous and sedimentary rocks into **metamorphic rocks**.

The forces change the rocks' minerals and textures. An example is limestone turning into marble.

marble

Metamorphic rocks
formed by heat
are called
contact rocks.

Those made by pressure are called **burial rocks**. **Regional rocks** are formed by both forces.

Rocks as Clues

Geologists study rocks to understand the world. Rocks tell about **climate** changes. They also show if a volcano erupted or if a lake was in an area.

Looking for Rocks

The beach is one of the best places to find rocks. All types of rocks wash up there. Most are smooth and small for picking!

Be a Geologist!

What you need:

**one igneous rock
(basalt or granite)**

**one sedimentary rock
(coal or limestone)**

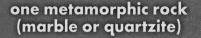

**one metamorphic rock
(marble or quartzite)**

**plastic containers big
enough for each rock**

1. Put each rock in its own container.

2. Fill each container with water.

3. Put the containers in the freezer.

4. Wait for the water to freeze. Then take the containers out to thaw.

5. Look at each rock to see which has changed the most.

Glossary

burial rocks—metamorphic rocks formed by pressure; burial rocks form deep underground.

climate—the common weather conditions in an area

contact rocks—metamorphic rocks formed by heat; contact rocks often form near magma.

erupts—bursts in an explosive way

geologists—scientists who study the earth

igneous rocks—rocks formed by lava or magma

lava—hot, melted rock that comes out of volcanoes

magma—hot, melted rock below the earth's surface

metamorphic rocks—rocks changed by heat, pressure, or both

minerals—solid substances found in nature

plutonic rocks—igneous rocks formed underground

regional rocks—metamorphic rocks formed by both heat and pressure

sedimentary rocks—rocks formed by material on the bottom of a body of water or in a desert

sediments—materials that settle on the bottom of a body of water or in a desert

solids—substances that keep their shape and volume

volcanic rocks—igneous rocks formed on the surface of the earth by cooled lava

volcanoes—holes in the earth; when a volcano erupts, lava shoots out.

To Learn More

AT THE LIBRARY
Hand, Carol. *Experiments with Rocks and Minerals.*
New York, N.Y.: Children's Press, 2012.

Rocks and Minerals: Facts at Your Fingertips. New
York, N.Y.: DK Pub., 2012.

Zoehfeld, Kathleen Weidner. *Rocks and Minerals.*
Washington, D.C.: National Geographic, 2012.

ON THE WEB
Learning more about rocks
is as easy as 1, 2, 3.

1. Go to www.factsurfer.com.

2. Enter "rocks" into the search box.

3. Click the "Surf" button and you will see a
   list of related web sites.

With factsurfer.com, finding more
information is just a click away.

Index

The images in this book are reproduced through the courtesy of: Igor Plotnikov, front cover; Pavel L Photo and Video, p. 4; John Hoffman, p. 5; OlegSam, pp. 6 (top), 8 (right); Tyler Boyes, pp. 6 (left), 10; Dr Ajay Kumar Singh, p. 6 (right); Webspark, p. 7; LoopAll, pp. 8, 14; Jon Eppard, p. 9; beboy, p. 11; Pierre Leclerc, p. 12; Supot Suebwongsa, p. 13; Fablok, p. 15; Steffen Foerster, p. 16; My Good Images, p. 17; Robert Garvey/ Corbis, p. 18; Robbie Shone/ Science Source, p. 19; First Light/ Glow Images, p. 20; michal812, p. 20 (top left); J. Schelkle, p. 20 (top right); Siim Sepp, p. 20 (bottom left); Africa Studio, p. 20 (bottom right).